O9-BTJ-195

A PLACE CALLED
HEARTBREAK
A STORY OF VIETNAM

by Walter Dean Myers
Alex Haley, General Editor

Illustrations by
Frederick Porter

RSVP
**RAINTREE
STECK-VAUGHN**
PUBLISHERS
The Steck-Vaughn Company

Austin, Texas

Published by Steck-Vaughn Company.

Text, illustrations, and cover art copyright © 1993 by Dialogue Systems, Inc., 627 Broadway, New York, New York 10012.
All rights reserved.

Cover art by Leonard Jenkins

Printed in the United States of America
    2 3 4 5 6 7 8 9 R 98 97 96 95 94

Library of Congress Cataloging-in-Publication Data

Myers, Walter Dean, 1937–
    A place called heartbreak: a story of Vietnam/by Walter Dean
Myers; illustrator, Frederick Porter.
        p.   cm.—(Stories of America)
    Summary: Describes the ordeal of Major Fred Cherry, who was
shot down in combat over Vietnam and spent seven-and-a-half
years as a prisoner of war in Hanoi.
        ISBN 0-8114-7237-X (hardcover) — ISBN 0-8114-8077-1 (pbk.)
        1. Vietnamese Conflict. 1961–1975—Prisoners and prisons.
North Vietnamese—Juvenile literature. 2. Cherry, Fred V.—
Juvenile literature. 3. Prisoners of war—United States—Juvenile
literature. 4. Prisoners of war—Vietnam—Juvenile literature.
[1. Vietnamese Conflict, 1961–1975—Prisoners and prisons, North
Vietnamese. 2. Cherry, Fred V. 3. Prisoners of war.] I. Porter,
Frederick, ill. II. Title. III. Series.
DS559.4.M94   1993
959.704'37—dc20   92-14428
                                                          CIP
                                                          AC

ISBN 0-8114-7237-X (Hardcover)
ISBN 0-8114-8077-1 (Softcover)

Introduction
by Alex Haley, General Editor

During the Gulf War in 1991, I found it odd that football players getting ready for a big playoff game described the upcoming contest as a "war." At the same time, I couldn't help but notice how some journalists reported the war as if *it* was a sporting event. I can even remember one journalist saying after the ground fighting brought the war near its close, "It's over. All that remains is to see how high we run up the score."

We need to be smarter than that. Warfare is not a game. It's a life-or-death struggle where "scores" are kept not in points or runs but in dead bodies, lost limbs, and damaged souls. *A Place Called Heartbreak* tells you about one man's experience among the routine horrors of war. It is not a sports report. It doesn't pretend war is pretty or fun or a game. It's a war story.

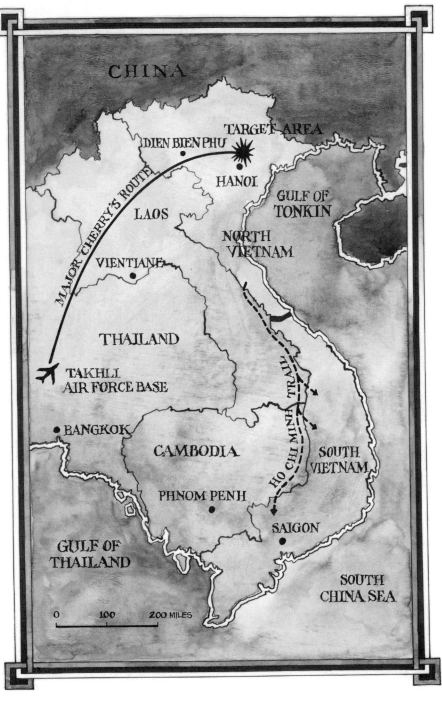

Contents

Chapter 1 What He Always
Wanted to Do   **1**

Chapter 2 Heading Out   **7**

Chapter 3 A Small Explosion   **18**

Chapter 4 A Question of Status   **23**

Chapter 5 This Was the War   **34**

Chapter 6 Prison Mercy   **42**

Chapter 7 The Prospect of
Freedom   **54**

Epilogue   **63**

Afterword   **67**

Notes   **67**

1

What He Always Wanted to Do

The sky had just lightened and already it was hot. An overhead fan hummed quietly as the two Air Force officers studied the colored maps before them.

"They've been building missile bases here," the senior officer said, tapping the map on the desk. "We want to knock them out as soon as we can."

He was talking to Major Fred V. Cherry. The major's flight suit was unzipped, but that didn't help much against the heat. It was usually hot in Thailand, and Takhli Air Force Base was no exception.

Major Cherry nodded and made mental notes to himself about the flight. He would have to refuel in midair or he wouldn't have enough fuel to return.

"What do they have up there?" he asked.

"Who knows?" The senior officer shrugged. "As far as we can tell, the North Vietnamese are just setting it up. I wouldn't take any chances, though."

"I'll try not to, sir," Major Cherry answered drily.

As he folded up the map, the slim fighter pilot let his mind wander. It was October 22, 1965. Back home, the Los Angeles Dodgers had just beaten the Minnesota Twins in a great World Series, and the heavyweight champion of the world was a kid named Muhammad Ali. *The Sound of Music* was the big movie, and Frank Sinatra was knocking them dead with his records. But back home was halfway round the world from Thailand.

Through the window he saw a group of pilots heading toward him. Major Cherry checked his watch. It was time for the preflight briefing.

The men who were to fly with him were good pilots, the best in the world. They didn't need a pep talk. All they had to know was where

the targets were and what kind of resistance to expect.

Cherry was leading the flight. It was his responsibility to tell the men what to expect.

"We can count on the usual ground fire," he said to the pilots. "There haven't been any reports of MIGs[1] in the area, but keep your eyes open anyway."

"Sounds routine," a lanky pilot said, leaning against a file cabinet.

"They all sound routine when we're standing in here," Major Cherry said. "But that doesn't mean it will be. Let's go do it."

The other pilots were out of the door first, with Cherry a step behind them. He stopped at the doorway, took a deep breath, and then went back into his office.

It was supposed to be standard operating procedure to empty your pockets before a flight. Leave everything behind that the enemy could use against you in case you were shot down. Cherry usually didn't follow the standard procedure, but somehow this day felt different.

He took his wallet from his pocket, glanced inside at the pictures of his children, and put it

---

[1] *enemy jet fighter planes*

4

in his desk drawer. There was a funny feeling in the pit of his stomach that lasted for a long moment, then was gone.

The F-105 jet bombers sitting on the runway had been checked by the flight crews. There would be four guys on the mission with him, one in each plane—four guys with families and loved ones back in the States. He watched as they carefully checked their gear. He took his revolver from his holster and checked it.

A young corporal checked the jet bomber's weapons and gave Cherry a snappy salute. "You're loaded to the teeth, sir," he said.

Cherry returned the salute and walked around his plane. He checked his plane visually, as he had for years as a pilot for the United States Air Force. The 750-pound bombs mounted under the wings seemed huge. Huge and deadly. The 2.5-inch rockets near the outer wings were thin and dart-shaped. The nose of the plane tapered to a sharp point.

Cherry closed the zippers on his flight suit and climbed into the cockpit. He plugged into the communication system and checked in with the tower. The tower gave him the weather report. He smiled when he heard that it was hot and muggy. What else was new?

Major Cherry lowered the canopy and gave the thumbs-up sign to the flight crew. He took a deep breath. In a moment he had revved up the powerful jet engine. The other pilots checked in. They were ready. They had clearance from the tower and taxied into takeoff positions.

"Let's do it!" Major Cherry said into the radio.

The jet shook slightly as it powered up. Then it moved quickly forward. In a moment Cherry was pressed against the back of the seat. The jet roared down the runway and lifted quickly into the blue-gray sky, the force of the lift pushing him harder against the back of his seat. They were on their way.

In the sky over Thailand there was a feeling of peace. If he looked straight ahead it was almost as if he wasn't moving. The lush, green jungles rushed by below. Cherry checked his course settings and relaxed. He was doing what he had always wanted to do—flying a combat mission for the United States Air Force.

2

Heading Out

Fred Cherry remembered his days as a teenager in Virginia. Sometimes, on clear days, when he and the other kids were playing in the school yard someone would point to the skies. The navy fighter pilots would be training there. He would stop whatever he was doing to watch them. He would watch them fly in tight formations, then peel off in mock battles. Fred would watch them twist and turn, the sun reflecting off their glass cockpits, and know that more than anything else in the world he wanted to fly.

He wanted to fly. He thought about flying and dreamt about flying, imagining how the pilots felt. He imagined their conversations as they talked back and forth during combat.

There were eight children in the Cherry family, four boys and four girls. Fred saw the heavy work that his father did. The head of the Cherry family always had at least two jobs, but Fred never heard him say a word about how hard things were.

Things were easier around the house when his mother could stay home, but that wasn't always possible. It wasn't the way he liked it, but that's the way it was. He knew what his parents were doing. They were trying to improve the whole family's chances for success. They were working hard, sacrificing, doing whatever it took to make things better.

All the children were expected to pitch in, to do their part to make things work. There weren't any crybabies in the Cherry household. You did what you were supposed to do, you did it well, and you didn't complain. During the week the children were expected to study and to help with the chores. On Sundays they were expected to go to church.

Neither of his parents had been able to go to high school, but they wanted their children to stay in school. Fred had to walk to East Suffolk High School every day. In winter the weather in Virginia was often very cold. In the late spring it

9

was so hot that the three miles back and forth to school seemed twice as long.

"Some things you can change and some things you just got to put up with," Fred's father said. "It's up to you to figure out which is which."

His father died before Fred finished high school. Losing his father was hard. Without the money his father earned, his mother had a difficult time supporting the children who were still living at home. To make it easier on his mother, Fred went to live with his married sister. Fred's sister had great faith in Fred's intelligence and his determination to succeed. He could grow up to be the first doctor in the family, she thought. All he had to do was to study hard and stay in school.

The idea of being a doctor was a good one, Fred thought. But it wasn't flying. And even though he entered Virginia Union University thinking he would one day be a doctor, he couldn't get his mind off flying. At the end of his four years at Virginia Union, he had to decide what he would do with his life. It was an easy decision. He was twenty-three years old when he joined the United States Air Force in 1951.

Flight school was tough. They said that they made it that way because they wanted only the best. All right, he thought. If they wanted the best then he would be the best. He wasn't as large as some of the other pilots, but he was as strong, as determined.

On the day that he received his wings as an Air Force pilot, a general was talking about what was happening in East Asia. Korea had been divided into two nations, North Korea and South Korea, after World War II. In June 1950, North Korea invaded South Korea. The United Nations sent soldiers to Korea to restore the peace. Many of those soldiers were Americans.

"Our guys," the general continued, "are facing highly trained Communist pilots flying Russian MIGs, one of the deadliest planes ever built."

These were the planes the young Fred Cherry flew against once he reached Korea in 1952. In Korea he flew an F-89G fighter bomber. Hurtling through the air at hundreds of miles per hour, with enemy planes and anti-aircraft gunners trying desperately to shoot him from the skies, he realized that any mission might be his last.

He was hit by ground fire a number of times, only once seriously. He was on a bombing mission, his plane still armed. He felt the hit and held his breath to see how the plane would react. If the hit was serious he knew the plane could blow up at any moment. Maybe it was only a light hit, but maybe he would have to bail out over Korea.

The plane began to act oddly, and he knew something was seriously wrong. The plane's tailpipe was on fire! If the fire reached the canisters of napalm he was carrying, it would be all over. The plane would explode.

He took the plane up as quickly as he could. Fire needs oxygen in order to burn. The higher Fred Cherry flew his plane, the thinner the oxygen was in the air. He was tense as the plane soared higher and higher through the air. Finally the oxygen was thin enough to put the fire out. Still, he didn't relax completely until he had returned to base and safely landed the fighter.

By the time a United Nations truce ended the Korean War in 1953, the young jet pilot was a veteran. Fred Cherry had flown fifty-three missions against the enemy.

The next few years Cherry spent in the peacetime Air Force. As a veteran pilot, he helped train the younger fliers. He knew that the United States was sending advisors to South Vietnam, a nation in Southeast Asia. But they weren't sending pilots. Not yet, anyway. Then, in 1964, Fred Cherry was once again asked to fight for his country. He was sent first to Karot Air Force Base in Thailand and from there to Takhli Air Force Base. It was from Takhli that Major Cherry was leading his mission now.

"I had no problems with the orders to go to Vietnam," he said. "The people in South Vietnam wanted to be free to make their own decisions. And being a serviceman, when the Commander in Chief says time to go, we head out."

Cherry liked the F-105. He liked the size of the sleek plane. It had good range, meaning it could fly nearly 1,800 miles between refuelings, and was the fastest tactical plane the Air Force had.

The F-105, and the pilots who flew it, specialized in air raids over North Vietnam. The official nickname of the plane was the Thunderchief, but the pilots often called the big plane the Thud.

Five Thuds streaked through the sky this October day in 1965. Major Fred Cherry was leading them in a routine air raid.

He was confident in the planes. He looked up at his wingman, flying just ahead and above him. Looking good. Everything was on schedule. It was at times like these, flying in formation over friendly skies, that flying was like living out a dream.

He felt good in the air. He loved flying, loved to see the canopy of sky overhead, loved to feel the embrace of the large plane as it powered him through the skies. He checked the other planes in his squadron again. He was leading the mission; it was his responsibility to see that everything went smoothly.

The radio crackled in his ears. Snatches of conversation from distant ships drifted in and quickly faded. He checked his watch. They were on schedule. It would be another twenty minutes before they reached the midair rendezvous with the refueling tankers.

They had already left Thailand's airspace and were now over Laos. They would refuel over Laos to make sure they had enough juice left for the return trip. Everything was smooth as silk.

Still, there was *something*, a slight tension that he hadn't felt on other missions. He tried to put it out of his mind.

He heard his code name being used on the radio. The tankers were approaching his group. He scanned the sky briefly and found them.

One by one the smaller fighter bombers lined up with the huge refueling tankers. In midair they found the nozzles, carefully nudged the planes onto them, and took on fuel. It went smoothly. No problems. Still, Cherry felt just a twinge of something. It wasn't fear. He wasn't afraid. It was just a feeling, a feeling that had come over him when he was first told about the mission that morning.

It felt good to roll away from the tankers. Hooked into the large refueling planes, he always felt like more of a target. He checked the flight plan and adjusted his course toward North Vietnam.

He checked his bearings. They were getting close to the area covered by North Vietnamese radar. There would be a warning light on the control panel when they were being picked up by radar, but he didn't want to wait that long before taking action.

"Let's take her down." He spoke calmly into the built-in mike. The lead plane dipped a wing and sliced downward through the still air. He knew the North Vietnamese radar was blocked by the mountains. The jets flew below the mountaintops, weaving around them. He began searching for ground features—rivers, hills, or buildings—that would tell him exactly where they were.

3

A Small Explosion

Just before them were the hills of Dien Bien Phu. In these hills the French had fought against the Vietnamese Communists after World War II. It was here that the French had suffered their final defeat.

The five jets slipped lower. Cherry was the leader; his plane was lower than the others, so he could keep an eye on them. Every nerve, every muscle was alert as he skimmed across the treetops.

He could hear his own breathing in his headset. His breath came faster and faster.

Cherry took his hand from the control stick and stretched his fingers. The American planes flew just above the ground for ten minutes, for fifteen minutes, for thirty minutes. The ground rushed under him at over five hundred miles per hour. He was low enough to see flashes of gunfire from the ground. He hoped they were aiming directly at him. If they aimed right at the huge plane, it would be long gone before the bullets reached it. But if they shot far enough ahead of the plane, he just might run into the path of the bullets.

Ahead of him he saw an odd-shaped compound. It was the missile base.

"On target!" he announced.

Now there was no turning back; nothing could stop the mission. The planes rushed for the missile sites. They had been spotted by ground troops. In a matter of seconds, the troops at the missile sites would know they were coming. But seconds were all that they would need.

Suddenly there was a loud clunk! It was the unmistakable sound of metal slamming into metal. He was hit! Still there was no turning back.

"On target!" he spoke sharply into the headset.

He kept his eyes straight ahead. He didn't want to run into a tall tree. Automatically he reached for the switches that would turn off part of the electrical system. He turned them off quickly. If there was an electrical fire, he didn't want it to spread. He wouldn't need the hydraulic system for the moment, and he turned that off, too.

He was still on target. Closer. Closer. There was the smell of smoke in the cockpit. Closer. Now!

He fired the bombs, holding the plane on target for another long second to make sure he didn't throw the bombs off course, then rolled the big plane over and away from the target site. He felt the plane straining skyward.

"Let's get out of here!" he barked into the radio.

Smoke began to pour from behind the instrument panel. There was a small explosion. The plane shook violently. He felt it turning out of control. His hands gripped the controls tightly as he tried desperately to straighten out the bomber. The cockpit was filling with thick, choking smoke.

There was another jolt. Was he hit again? The plane spun crazily through the air. He couldn't tell whether he was right side up or not. Seconds were all he had to get out of the plane before it either crashed or blew up completely. He pulled on the controls, trying to bring the jet's nose up. He had to get the nose up for an instant if he was going to eject. Just for an instant.

The plane seemed to groan as it strained upward. He couldn't see. As soon as he felt the plane responding and sensed that the nose was going up, he hit the ejection controls. The cockpit cover flew open and he was literally shot from the top of the plane. He was spinning through the air, trying to get his bearings.

He realized he was still strapped into his seat. He found the rip cord and pulled it. The parachute began to open with a rush. He saw the dark form of his wingman's plane against the sky. He tried to look down. Seconds later he was slamming into the ground.

His whole body shook from the impact as he rolled over and over.

4

A Question of Status

The United States had been involved in the war against North Vietnam since the early 1950s. At first Congress had approved only money and supplies to help the French and then, after Dien Bien Phu, the South Vietnamese. But by 1954 American soldiers were advising the South Vietnamese. A year later, the first Americans died in Vietnam.

As time went on, the number of American troops in Vietnam slowly increased. By 1961 there were three thousand American troops in Vietnam. The numbers began rising faster.

In 1962 there were eleven thousand American soldiers in Vietnam.

In 1963 the number of American soldiers in Vietnam had reached sixteen thousand.

By 1964, the year that Fred Cherry was assigned to an Air Force base in Thailand, over twenty thousand American soldiers were in Vietnam. And their role was changing, too. They were no longer just advising; now they were fighting. The death toll was rising slowly but surely. Still the United States was not officially "at war" with Vietnam.

Then, in the summer of 1964, an incident occurred off the eastern coast of North Vietnam that would be the center of controversy for a long time. It would also be an important incident to Fred Cherry.

On August 2, 1964, in the Gulf of Tonkin, a destroyer belonging to the United States reported that it was fired upon by North Vietnamese patrol boats. Two days later the ship returned to the same area, this time with another destroyer. It reported that it was again fired upon. In response to these reports, the President of the United States, Lyndon B. Johnson, presented a special resolution to Congress.

It was called the Southeast Asia Resolution, and it said that the Communist government of North Vietnam had attacked American ships. It went on to say that the attacks were part of a campaign against the United States and against North Vietnam's neighbors in Southeast Asia.

The resolution stated that "Congress approves and supports the determination of the President, as Commander in Chief, to take all necessary measures to repel any armed attack against the forces of the United States and to prevent further aggression."

In addition, the resolution allowed the President the power "to take all necessary steps, including the use of armed force" to assist any nation friendly to the United States that asked the President for help.

This resolution was passed in the House of Representatives by a vote of 416 to 0. In the Senate, it passed by a vote of 88 to 2. Only two members of Congress opposed the Southeast Asia Resolution.

But to some people there was a major problem with it. The problem was this: according to the Constitution, only Congress has the power to declare war. The Southeast Asia Resolution, while *not* a declaration of war, gave President Johnson the go-ahead to fight a war. Was this legal? Some Americans thought it wasn't.

But with the passage of this resolution, the

United States became completely committed to a combat role in Vietnam.

It was a strange way for the United States to enter a war. And while it proved troubling to an increasing number of Americans, most Americans in 1964 felt as Fred Cherry did: ". . . when the Commander in Chief says time to go, we head out."

━━━━━━

Fred Cherry had responded to his President's call, and now he found himself shot down over North Vietnam, a few miles from Hanoi.

He looked up from where he was sitting and saw a dozen, perhaps more, North Vietnamese. Some wore uniforms; most did not. There were rifles pointed at him by the ones in uniform. Some of the men and women were clearly farmers. They had grabbed their farm tools and come out to see what had dropped from the sky.

Fred Cherry's pistol was visible to the Vietnamese. One of the soldiers motioned for him to raise his arms. He tried, but only one arm moved. There wasn't any pain in his left arm; it just didn't move. A man motioned for him to raise his left arm. Cherry looked at the rifle pointed at his chest and swallowed hard.

He made another effort to lift his arm, but couldn't. He pointed toward his left shoulder and shook his head. The Vietnamese understood that he had been wounded. They approached him carefully. One took the pistol and his hunting knife. Another tried to get his flight suit off.

Cherry wondered what they had in mind for him. He wondered whether they would kill him. He could picture them shooting him or even hacking him to death with the farm tools they carried. He licked his lips nervously.

They motioned for him to stand, and he rocked forward onto his knees. As he stood he felt a pain in his left ankle. Someone pushed him with a stick. He was to go along a path.

He had heard the Vietnamese language before, even understood a few words, but he couldn't understand these people as they laughed and talked among themselves.

He was suddenly very tired. He limped along the road as best he could. He thought about dying, about being buried in a strange country.

Children came behind him and touched him. He tried to smile at them. They giggled. One of the young men in uniform seemed to be in charge. That made Cherry feel better. He was counting on his status as a prisoner of war and felt that another soldier, even an enemy soldier, would understand and respect that status.

As they approached a village, he heard a gong. The gong was calling out the villagers to see the prize. His ankle was hurting more, but he tried to ignore it. He had to keep his wits about him.

They marched him into a village and then along a road. One of the soldiers put a cloth over Cherry's white T-shirt to make him harder to spot from the air. In the distant sky two American jets made slow passes as they searched for him. There was a beeper in his parachute, and they were homing in on its location.

The Vietnamese pushed him into a rice paddy. Someone sat on him and pushed the muzzle of an automatic weapon against the bone behind his ear. He wondered what it would take for the man to pull the trigger.

The rice paddy was cold and deep. The shoulder that he couldn't lift was now beginning to hurt, and his wrist was injured. He kept his head down. They hadn't killed him yet. Maybe, he thought, just maybe, they wouldn't.

Fred Cherry felt the cold pressure of the gun muzzle suddenly relax. Then he found himself being yanked to his feet by the man who had just been sitting on him. He was pushed forward. They marched out of the paddy and onto a path that led into another village.

The furniture in the building they took him into was small, and he thought that possibly it was a school. They put a chair in front of a desk and pushed him into it. A guard with an automatic weapon stood behind him.

The questions were in fairly good English.

"Cherry, Fred V., Major!" he answered. He added his serial number and date of birth. His mind went back to the instructions he had received during his training: if captured by the enemy, give only your name, rank, serial number, and date of birth.

The soldier asking the questions responded angrily. He spoke sharply in Vietnamese, and the guard behind Cherry hit him with his fist.

There was another question.

"Cherry, Fred V., Major!"

This time the blow was harder, nearly knocking him off the chair. A soldier on his right lifted his weapon and pointed it at him. Cherry could feel his heart beating in his chest. He tightened his lips and swallowed.

The pain in his left shoulder and wrist came in great waves. He knew that his wrist was broken and that something was dreadfully wrong with his shoulder. His ankle might also have been broken, but he wasn't sure of that yet. He was just sure that it wouldn't stop hurting.

He wanted to say something about the Geneva Conventions, but the words didn't come. The Geneva Conventions were a set of rules concerning the treatment of soldiers and civilians during war. Most of the world's nations agreed to them. They said that countries must treat prisoners of war humanely, must supply information about the status of prisoners, and must permit visits to the prison camps by representatives from neutral countries.

"You are a criminal!" the North Vietnamese soldier said in slow, precise English.

Major Cherry took a deep breath. He had heard the arguments about the legality of the war before. He wasn't sure about the details, but he knew that he wouldn't win an argument with the angry man who sat across from him.

To Fred Cherry and the men who fought

with him, the legality of the war was not a question. They were soldiers fighting for their country, fighting for freedom, fighting to stop Communism. Besides, their representatives in Congress had passed the Southeast Asia Resolution that allowed the President to send them to Vietnam.

But how the North Vietnamese treated their prisoners would depend not on how Americans viewed the war's legal issues but on how the North Vietnamese viewed them.

Cherry was again pulled to his feet. He almost fainted from the pain when his arms were suddenly forced behind him and tied tightly behind his back. He was pushed out of the building.

Outside, a crowd of villagers had gathered around to see him—men in simple peasant dress with farm tools, some with rifles, an incredibly pretty girl carrying a baby. A young Vietnamese farmer ran up to him and rubbed his skin to see if the color would come off. The farmer was quickly chased away by the soldiers.

Just beyond the villagers, Cherry saw an old, battered, quarter-ton truck. He was led to it and lifted on. Two guards sat with him in the back. Major Fred Cherry was the forty-third American captured in North Vietnam, and the first American black. He said a silent prayer as the truck lurched away from the village.

5

This Was the War

From the outside, Hoa Lo Prison didn't look very much like a prison at all. Its antique gates looked as if they might lead to a private estate or mansion. Its white walls, although discolored by age, looked like the walls of some tropical resort hotel. In fact, American prisoners called the prison the Hanoi Hilton.

Inside the gates there were few guards. Several civilian workers stopped to look at Cherry. Some moved closer as he was pushed along the walk. The trees in the courtyard were tall, almost majestic. They would have been beautiful in Virginia.

The walk leading to the house had a fancy cobblestone design that looked as if it had been there for decades. A steel cover in the middle of the walk probably provided access to a primitive draining system. There wouldn't be many of the comforts of home.

Major Cherry was taken into a room and shoved toward a chair. He recognized the setup: a rickety wooden chair in front of a large desk. It was just like the room in the village. Only the furniture was bigger. The man with his back toward the desk would probably be his questioner.

He sat down. The chair was close to the desk—so close that there was just barely room for his knees. The pain in his shoulder was worse, but he refused to give in to it. His interrogator[2] would use any weakness, he knew. He needed something to distract himself. He noticed a plant in a large urn against the stucco wall. It was well cared for. He tried to keep his mind on it.

The man facing the wall turned toward him. He looked Cherry over carefully. Cherry

---

[2] *questioner*

looked back at him, trying not to show the pain he felt, or how tired he was.

"What was your mission?" The question was asked in a flat, even tone.

"Cherry, Fred V., Major!"

The chair was jolted from under him. The pain seared through his body as he crashed to the floor. In seconds he had been picked up and placed back on the chair. He looked at the Vietnamese officer in front of him.

"What was your mission?" the officer asked again, just as evenly as before.

"Cherry, Fred V., Major!"

He tried to tense his body before the chair was kicked out from under him again. It didn't help much.

He was on the chair again, and the questions continued.

"You killed thirty people," the officer said, with anger seeping into his voice for the first time. "Do you feel good about that?"

"I didn't kill anybody," Cherry said. "I just gather information."

"What kind of a plane did you fly?"

"An R-105 reconnaissance plane," Cherry said.

The officer wrote the information down. "What was your destination?"

"I don't know," Cherry said. "The plane is guided automatically. I just push the buttons and—"

A hand grabbed the back of his head and smashed it into the desk.

"What was your destination?" the officer asked again. He spread maps out on the desk. Cherry could tell, even upside down, that they were his maps. They had been taken from the downed plane.

He sat for a while without answering the question. The officer looked up at him. Cherry tried to think of something to say, but it was already too late. The chair was kicked out from under him again, and he went crashing to the floor. He was then picked up again and put back on the chair.

"Who was in your squadron?"

He knew the game now. They would give him all the pain he could take. He would either have to take it or break. He decided that he wouldn't break. He tried to think of other things, tried to put himself mentally in other places. He imagined that he was still flying,

maneuvering his plane against an enemy that he could fight, instead of sitting with his arms tied behind his back and a gun pointed at the back of his head.

He was punched several times around the ears and the top of the head. His ears rang and his nose was bleeding. He wasn't sure if the blood was from the punches or from having his head slammed into the desk.

"Under the Geneva Conventions . . ." he began, pausing to try and clear the blood from his throat "you can't treat a prisoner of war this way."

"You are not a prisoner of war!" The North Vietnamese officer stood up quickly. "You are a criminal!"

The questioning went on. So did the beating. He decided that he was ready to die. He might die, but he wouldn't break.

It was daybreak before they took him to a cell. They had kept him up all night. There wasn't a bed in the cell, just the concrete floor to lie upon. There were leg chains fastened into one wall. The doors were large and seemed solid except for the holes in the bottom. He lay on the floor, cold, tired, in agony from the beatings. This was Vietnam, he thought; this was war.

He hadn't expected a pleasant experience as a captive. He was a prisoner in North Vietnam, a country that he fought against, that he had dropped bombs on so many times.

He realized that no one knew that he was still alive, except these few Vietnamese. They could simply kill him if they wanted.

In a few hours the questions began again. They asked him questions about his plane, about his mission. Where had he flown from? What had his targets been? What did he know about the defenses of North Vietnam?

He refused to answer their questions.

"Cherry, Fred V., Major!" was all that he would give them.

They beat him. Calmly. Deliberately. His shoulder and arm had been badly hurt when he landed. They knew the pain he was in as they twisted his arms behind his back and pushed his hands up until they were almost to his head. They could see the sweat on his brow as the injured shoulder was almost pulled out of its joint. Then they tied his arms in that position. They walked away from him, had tea, chatted among themselves. He couldn't fight that kind of pain; he couldn't deny it. He just had to take it, for minutes, sometimes for hours. Eventually he would know the room only by its nickname, a place called Heartbreak. They were telling him something, and the message was clear. If he could keep up his stubborn resistance, they could keep up his pain. This was Vietnam; this was the war.

6

Prison Mercy

For the first few weeks each day was full of fear. Would they get tired of his refusal to answer? At night, instead of waking him for more questions, would they simply take him out and shoot him? In the past he had thought about being captured, but always in his imagination he had escaped, always he had managed to get back to his base.

The rainy October stretched into an even rainier November. Time in the Hanoi Hilton was passing slowly, but Fred Cherry thought he could handle it. Then one day he was bound and put into the back of a truck.

A thousand thoughts raced through his mind as he bounced along the dirt road. He tried to distract himself with questions that didn't have to do with where they were taking him or what might be coming next. Instead he wondered about the people in his squadron. What were they doing? Were they planning another raid? Were they thinking about him? Did they even know he was alive?

The mud-caked truck lurched along without stopping. The jolting hurt his shoulder, and he tried to lean against the side of the truck for support. Finally the truck stopped, and he was told to get out. His legs were shaky as he looked around. It was another prison camp.

Cu Loc Prison was a lot like the Hanoi Hilton. The cells were small; the air was hot and smelly. The beatings were the same, and so were the questions.

"Why do you defend your country when they treat you like a slave?" he was asked. "Help us. We will treat you well."

"I am black," Major Cherry answered. "*And I am American.*"

He didn't have a chance to get ready for the blow. For a moment his head spun from its force. He tried not to look at his captors. There was no use in staring at them, making them think he was being defiant.

"Why do you not admit that you are a criminal?" he was asked.

He knew the next blow would come. They would beat him unless he agreed to cooperate with them. He didn't answer, and his face was pushed down onto the desk in front of him.

The questions and the beatings went on day after day. He had been counting the days he was being held. Now he just counted the days he was being beaten.

At the end of each day's beating, he would be carried, sometimes dragged, back to his cell and dropped onto the floor. Ninety-two days of beatings went slowly by.

They put another flier, a naval officer, in the cell with him. Cherry was in such pain that he could hardly talk to the man. Sometimes, when the fever from his infected shoulder was very high, he could hear himself talking and tried to shut himself up. He didn't trust his new cellmate. Sometimes, in the agony and the pain from the beatings, he didn't even trust himself.

———

The days stretched into weeks. The weeks stretched into months.

"I will live through this," he told himself. "I will live through this."

They had put a cast on his broken ankle. It should have been taken off after a few weeks. Before long, it began to itch. When the itch turned into a burning, he knew the skin under the cast was infected.

"You have to take it off," he told his captors.

For a long time his pleas were ignored. He began to lose weight and had trouble remaining conscious. His captors decided, finally, to remove the cast.

They put him on a stretcher and took him into one of the rooms they used as a hospital. It was March 18, 1966. He had been a prisoner for nearly five months.

A Vietnamese medic cut through the dirty cast. There was pain as the infected skin stuck to the bandage. Cherry closed his eyes and clenched his teeth. The smell from the infection was terrible.

One of the Vietnamese medics looking at his badly infected ankle issued a command. One of the others left the room.

Cherry tried to lift his head to see how bad the leg was. It was bad. The medics would have to operate. The one who had left returned with what looked like a beer bottle. When he took the stopper off the bottle, the smell filled the room. It was gasoline!

When they began pouring the gasoline onto the open sores of his leg, it took his breath away. His whole body shook as the room filled with gas fumes. The pain was unbearable. The room seemed to darken. . . .

As he came to, he felt someone slapping the arteries in his arm. He opened his eyes and saw the Vietnamese medic staring intently into his face. The medic seemed to relax when he saw that Cherry was still alive.

Yes, Cherry thought, *I am alive, and I will live through this. I will live through this.*

On the tenth of April, he was operated on again, this time on his injured shoulder. After the operation they put him in a small room by himself. He had never felt so alone.

Two Vietnamese girls were assigned to clean the hospital rooms. They were teenagers. The two girls brought him candy and fruit. One would look out for the guards while the other one gave him the food. Even in the presence of his enemies, even in prison, there was mercy. He would live through it.

The days in the prison hospital were not too bad—there were no beatings. Perhaps, he thought, the worst was over. But then he was taken from the hospital back to a cell, and the beatings resumed. By July Cherry was back in the hospital. After a month's stay he was returned to his cell. There were more beatings. It was a routine of torture, a routine of suffering. Fred Cherry began spitting up blood in his cell and was back in the hospital in November. This time he stayed there for months. When doctors finally operated on him, it was May 1967. They removed a rib and a number of bone chips from his chest.

One day soon after the operation, a guard tried to make Cherry get out of bed and mop the floor. It would have killed him. A Vietnamese nurse prevented it. Instead she mopped the floor for Fred Cherry. She also snuck extra food into his room. His condition improved and he was once again returned to his cell.

He was alone. The days seemed longer when he was alone. He counted the days. Two, three, four, five days alone. Then weeks alone. Then months. He would be alone in his cell for almost a year.

When, at long last, he was put into a cell

with other American prisoners, he was filled with joy. To see a friendly human being, to hear a friendly voice, was just wonderful. The interrogations continued but the beatings let up. Slowly Cherry grew stronger.

Some of the new men coming into the prison weren't doing well. When they asked him how long he had been in the Zoo—that was what they called Cu Loc Prison—he told them that he had been a prisoner since October 1965.

The fact that he had been there that long— over three years now—was discouraging to some of the men. It was discouraging to Cherry, too.

He wanted to know what was going on back in the United States. He wanted to know how the war was going, but it was more than that. He wanted to know what was happening in the World that he had come from. That was what the men in the service called life back in the States—the World.

What was going on in the World was not very pleasant. Fred Cherry had heard that Martin Luther King, Jr., had been assassinated, and Bobby Kennedy, too. He had heard about the anti-war protests on college campuses across the country. His captors had told him these things during interrogation sessions, but he never believed them. Now the new guys were telling him. They also told him about the war.

It was hard to tell from inside the prison camp how the war was going. The North Vietnamese had launched a series of attacks during Tet, the Vietnamese New Year's holiday. The Tet Offensive, as it became known, failed. Each of the North Vietnamese attacks was beaten back. However, after Tet, American generals called for even more soldiers to be sent to Vietnam. Rather than coming to an end, the Vietnam War seemed to be growing. Despite the Tet victory, many people felt that the United States was losing the war.

The new guys arriving at the Zoo didn't seem as confident that the United States would win the war. Many wondered whether they would ever get home again.

Cherry knew that he would survive. He felt it in his bones. But that wasn't enough anymore. He had to help the others survive, too.

The Zoo was rough, but it wasn't the end of

the world. The prisoners who had been there longest helped the newcomers, even if it meant risking additional beatings. Cherry would do his best to get the new men into a routine that would help them to survive. He did it whenever a new prisoner was put into a cell next to his.

"Hey, new guy! You hear me?"

"Yeah."

"Listen, I'm Major Fred Cherry. This is the Tap Code. The alphabet has twenty-five letters, no *K*. Five lines of five letters. The first tap is for the line. The second tap is the letter in the line. Remember, no *K*. Use *C* for *K*."

A guard came over and started yelling and threatening Cherry. Cherry knew it might mean a beating when the guard got around to it. He took a deep breath, waited until the guard walked down the narrow corridor, and called the new prisoner again. They had to be able to communicate. There was no other way to learn what the newcomer knew. There was no other way to keep up each other's spirits.

"Look, it's simple. First tap is the line; the second tap is the letter in that line. What's this word?" *Tap tap—tap tap tap,* then *tap tap—tap tap tap tap?*

```
A B C D E
F G H I J
L M N O P
Q R S T U
V W X Y Z
```

"Let's see—second line, third letter—
H, then second line, fourth letter—*I*." The voice
that came back sounded young. "That's *Hi*."

"See, it's a piece of cake."

They went over the code again until Cherry
was sure the new prisoner had it. Once the code
was learned it could be used to tap messages
against the walls quietly enough so that the
guards couldn't hear.

The new guy in the next cell told Cherry he
had been shot down by a SAM—surface-to-air
missile. Like the other new guys, he brought
news of the outside world to the Zoo—news that
the Vietnamese didn't give them. The Boston
Celtics were the champs of the National Basket-
ball Association. *Rosemary's Baby* was playing
at the movies, and Richard Nixon was the new
President of the United States.

In 1969 there was a brief celebration when
news reached the prisoners that Americans had
landed on the moon. A couple of guys joked that

maybe they would land in Hanoi next. There was more talk about protests against the war. The protests were getting larger, and it wasn't only college kids who were taking part in them. All kinds of people were protesting now, even some guys who had fought in Vietnam.

Good or bad, the news from home didn't make it any easier.

7

The Prospect of Freedom

It was December 1970. The men at the Zoo had been rounded up and moved back to the Hanoi Hilton. At first nobody knew what had happened, and there were rumors that the war was winding down. Then they found out that there had been a raid by American Special Forces.[3] The raid was at a place called Son Tay. Son Tay was less than two hours by truck from Hanoi. The Special Forces guys had hit the base hard, fast, and about three months too late. The prisoners at the camp had already been moved.

---

[3] *highly-trained U.S. combat unit*

It had been five years since Fred Cherry had been at the Hilton. This time things were not quite as hard. His wounds had healed, and there were fewer beatings. Most of all there was more of a chance to be with the other men, and to get news from home.

Much of the news from home was bad. The news about Kent State wasn't just bad, it was terrible. Several of the new prisoners at the Hanoi Hilton knew about Kent State, and they told the others.

Kent State is a beautiful college in Kent, Ohio. The campus sprawls over a large area. The grass-covered grounds are neatly kept, and the paths arc free of litter. The campus was usually peaceful, but on May 4, 1970, there was a student demonstration.

It had just been revealed that President Nixon had sent American troops into Cambodia. President Nixon said that the North Vietnamese were using bases in Cambodia to prepare attacks on American forces in South Vietnam. New rounds of anti-war protests greeted the President's actions.

Many students at Kent State felt it was wrong for the United States to expand the war into Cambodia. Most of the students just milled about the campus, carrying signs or chanting their opposition to the war. Some surrounded the R.O.T.C.[4] building.

Worried that the demonstration might turn violent, the governor of Ohio summoned the National Guard to Kent State. Most of the young men in the National Guard were close in age to the students at Kent State. The two groups faced each other on that sunny May day. Then, for some reason, several of the National Guardsmen opened fire. Thirteen of the students were shot. Four were killed.

A week later there was a demonstration at Jackson State College in Mississippi. Two students were killed in that demonstration.

The men at Hoa Lo Prison—the Hanoi Hilton—were there because they had been captured while fighting for their country. They believed that what they were doing was right. They believed that the sacrifices they were making and all the years in prison were for the good of their country. They wanted to know that the country they were fighting for believed in them.

---

[4] *Many colleges have a Reserve Officer Training Corps where students receive some military training.*

Now it was clear that, at the very least, a lot of people no longer believed in the war.

Fred Cherry hadn't given up on the war. It was a war he still thought the United States and South Vietnam could win. It was a war that he, as an American, had risked his life to win. Sometimes he thought of ways the United States could win. They could bomb North Vietnam until they leveled the whole country.

Then he thought of the students at Kent State and Jackson State. They were protesting the war, and it was their right to do so. In a way it was strange: he had fought, had risked his life, for the right of other Americans to protest his fighting. It was a strange war.

It was 1971. Cherry was approaching his sixth year as a prisoner. He knew that peace talks had begun in Paris. The North Vietnamese boasted that the Americans were begging for peace. The American servicemen tried not to show any interest in the peace talks. They were captives, but they didn't want to give any comfort to the enemy.

For Cherry the peace talks meant that the war might soon be over and that he would be freed. But he wouldn't allow himself to get his hopes up. There was too much that might go wrong. While the beatings had all but stopped, the health conditions at the Hanoi Hilton were still bad. Many of the men had died from diseases. Cherry was still weak, still underweight. The food was bad and the sanitation terrible. He had to hang on.

Rumor had it that the peace talks were stalled while they argued about the shape of the table. Should it be round, square or oval? It was clear that they were not in a hurry. The captive Americans wished that their country would do something to speed up the process.

Then, on December 18, 1972, Hanoi was attacked by 126 American bombers.

Cherry sat quietly as the bombs fell within yards of the prison. Some of the men were singing; some congratulated each other. The American pilots knew where the prison was, and the captives just hoped that they would be accurate. The walls of the prison shook as the guards took cover. A choking dust swirled about the darkness.

At the peace talks, the United States was trying to get assurances that North Vietnam would not escalate the war if the United States withdrew. A month after the raid on Hanoi, an agreement was reached.

In January 1973, a Vietnamese officer stepped into the prison courtyard. He called for attention. He said that he had an important announcement. The Americans in the courtyard were playing cards or talking among themselves. They shuffled slowly into a loose formation before the officer. The Vietnamese officer read aloud the peace agreement that had been reached in Paris.

The Americans had expected it. Inside they were thrilled, but they still wouldn't let their captors know how glad they were at the prospect of freedom. They didn't cheer. They listened patiently and then went back to playing cards or checkers, leaving the Vietnamese officer standing alone in the middle of the yard.

On Monday, the twelfth of February, forty men were put on a bus and taken to the airport. They were the sickest men and the ones who had been prisoners the longest. Among this group was Major Fred Cherry. He had been a prisoner of war for nearly seven and a half years.

Cherry sat on the bus for what seemed like forever. Some of the men talked quietly among themselves. Others were alone with their thoughts. The thought that something might go wrong, that the bus would turn around and take them back to the Hanoi Hilton, was in all their minds.

"Here it comes!"

In the distance the dark profile of an American C-141 transport lumbered toward the runway. The men got out of the bus and lined up. Cherry watched the plane as it touched down and rolled to a stop. A Vietnamese car drove out to meet the plane. Cherry watched as the doors of the plane opened, straining his eyes until he recognized the uniforms of the men who were deplaning. They were American uniforms worn by the American officers sent to escort the prisoners home. A hundred thoughts now ran through Cherry's mind. He hoped the plane was in good condition. He hoped there wouldn't be any last-minute snags. He remembered it was Lincoln's birthday. But most of his thoughts were of freedom.

An American colonel came up to the prisoners and saluted the senior officer.

"Just a few more minutes, guys. Hang on," he said.

A few brief formalities, and then they would be free! Some of the escort officers had tears in their eyes as they embraced the waiting Americans. There were handshakes as they took seats on the C-141. As soon as the men were seated, the plane began to slowly taxi to the takeoff position. It began to roll; it picked up speed; it was in the air. He was flying.

The sound of the wheels folding into the well was the signal for the men to start cheering. They were free! They were going home—returning to the World.

There was a hometown parade for the newly promoted Colonel Fred Cherry. The parade filled him with pride as the people of Sussex, Virginia, came out to greet him and to thank him for his sacrifice. It had been a long, hard struggle, but he had survived. He had survived, and in a remarkable triumph of the will, he had survived with dignity and courage.

Epilogue

Today Fred Cherry is a successful marketing consultant in his native Virginia. He has renewed his friendship with some of the men who were prisoners with him for so long. He still thinks of the Vietnamese girls who helped him and wonders what happened to them. He's gained weight, but he still looks youthful.

He often thinks about his days as an American fighter pilot. He still thinks of his service to his country in Korea and Vietnam with pride. He will never forget his incredibly long imprisonment in North Vietnam. He believes that the American presence in Vietnam was correct, and that it was our determination as a nation and the sacrifices of our young people that stopped the spread of Communism in Southeast Asia.

"I don't know if we'll ever stop wars from being waged," he says. "And war is a miserable thing. But I would advise young people to think about wars and to do those things that will prevent them. The nine-year-olds of today are the leaders of the future. They have to prepare themselves not just to fight and win wars, but to stop them from ever happening."

Two million Americans served in Vietnam. The United States of America suffered the loss of 58,022 of its young people killed in Vietnam. Another 13,000 were totally disabled. Thousands more were killed in accidents during training or while serving in noncombat roles.

It is estimated that between a million and a million and a half Vietnamese lost their lives because of the war. And one hundred thousand Vietnamese were totally disabled as a result of the war.

The truce that allowed the United States to withdraw from the war did not last. Two years later, Saigon, the capital of South Vietnam, fell to North Vietnamese troops. Today Vietnam is one nation. It is a nation that still suffers from the political and economic wounds of the war.

In the United States, we are still in the process of healing our divisions. But we have seen the face of war and have learned, to some extent, how to think about it. Perhaps more importantly, we have learned that we can't leave the thinking about wars to other people. We must do our own thinking, and prepare ourselves, as Fred Cherry says, "not just to fight and win wars, but to stop them from ever happening."

Afterword

I've spent years trying to understand what happened to America both in Vietnam and back home in the World. I've talked to hundreds of veterans across the country. I've read the papers and books such as *Bloods* by Wallace Terry and *When Hell Was in Session* by U.S. Senator Jeremiah A. Denton, Jr.

But nowhere did the political experience of a nation and the personal experience of an individual come more to life for me than when I interviewed Colonel Fred V. Cherry about his experiences as an Air Force fighter pilot. His is one story of thousands that could be told about the Vietnam War, but it has helped me to understand the war a little better, as well as the people who fought it.

I would like to thank Colonel Cherry for his time and assistance in preparing this book.

Notes

Page 2 American warplanes leaving Thailand often flew a distance of over seven hundred miles to reach their targets in North Vietnam. They could cover such distances only by refueling their planes in mid-air as they neared Vietnam. For pilots like Colonel Cherry this created a very odd contrast between life on the base in Thailand and life in the air over Vietnam. They would fly into the war zone and face ferocious anti-aircraft fire, enemy fighter fire, and surface-to-air missiles. They would then attack their targets and return to bases completely removed from the war zone. Warplanes today have an even greater range. Some of the planes used in the Persian Gulf War in 1991 attacked targets in Iraq from bases in Great Britain.

Pages 11–12 The Korean War lasted from June 1950 to July 1953. The war, described as a "police action" by President Harry Truman, ended as it began, with Korea divided at the 38th Parallel. Some estimates of the total number of casualties in the Korean War reach almost five million people. Over fifty thousand Americans lost their lives in the Korean War.

Page 13 Vietnam has had a long and complex history, much of it a record of its struggle to be an independent nation. Its early history was a continuous battle against China, its northern neighbor. Before World War II, the French made Vietnam a part of its colonial empire. During World War II, it was occupied by the Japanese. When the war ended, Ho Chi Minh, a Vietnamese patriot and a Communist, appealed to the United States to aid Vietnam in its wish to be free from French colonialism. The United States, however, had adopted a Cold War policy of confronting the spread of Communism. In keeping with this policy, the United States sided with the French against Ho Chi Minh, setting the stage for United States involvement in the Vietnamese conflict.

Page 16 Fred Cherry's mission on October 22, 1965 required a round trip of 1,400 miles, a distance within the maximum flying range of the F-105. However, because something could go wrong—an enemy attack, a search for a downed companion, poor weather conditions—the planes refueled to make sure that there would be more than twenty minutes of reserve fuel.

Page 25 The Vietnam War became a very controversial war, but the passage of the Gulf of Tonkin Resolution by such an incredible majority of the Congress shows that support for United States involvement was strong in the beginning. Criticism grew slowly in scope and significance over the course of the war. It wasn't until the very end of the 1960s that many members of Congress and the mainstream news media began to question the wisdom of United States policy to win the war. It's been more than twenty years since our involvement in the war ended, and there is still little agreement about what went wrong in Vietnam.

Page 31 The Geneva Conventions are a set of agreements signed by most of the world's nations. They provide guidelines for the conduct of war and the humane treatment of prisoners of war. These conventions are often violated and generally unenforceable in negotiated settlements. In Vietnam, the Communists claimed that the "illegality" of the war removed them from the obligation to abide by the conventions. In the Persian Gulf War, Iraqi leaders claimed they were not subject to rules of the conventions when treating Allied pilots because those pilots had committed war crimes in bombing Iraqi cities and towns.

Pages 31–32 The legality of the Vietnam War has often been questioned. The Constitution of the United States gives Congress the exclusive power to declare war. Since World War II, however, there have been many incidents of war where Congress did not declare war before the President committed troops in a conflict.

Congress did not declare war in Korea. Nor did it declare war when it passed the Gulf of Tonkin Resolution in 1964, authorizing President Johnson to send combat troops to Vietnam. More recently the United States invaded Grenada (1983) and Panama (1990), and sent troops to Lebanon (1982–83) and the Persian Gulf (1991) without declarations of war.

Each of these engagements was seen as a "limited" action, but so too were both Korea and Vietnam at first. The President wants the freedom to respond to fast-developing crises; Congress, without surrendering its Constitutional powers and responsibilities, wants to cooperate, but the question remains troubling and unresolved.

Page 43 The North Vietnamese interrogators were aware of the Civil Rights movement in the United

States in which African Americans were attempting to end segregation and racial discrimination in the States. They also knew that the ancestors of most African Americans had been brought to America as slaves. They tried to use this to turn African-American prisoners against the United States.

In South Vietnam, where the ground war was fought, Communists often left special messages for African-American troops to try to convince them not to fight against a Third World nation like Vietnam when whites in America treated blacks as inferior citizens. This was an especially significant challenge because African-American soldiers made up a disproportionate percentage of the United States combat force. However, despite the harsh realities of prejudice at home, African Americans served their country with great loyalty and courage.

Walter Dean Myers is the author of numerous prize-winning books for children and young adults. Most recently, he received the 1992 Coretta Scott King Award for *Now Is Your Time! The African American Struggle for Freedom.*